THE RED PILL

An impassioned plea to America to wake up and be ready for the coming financial collapse

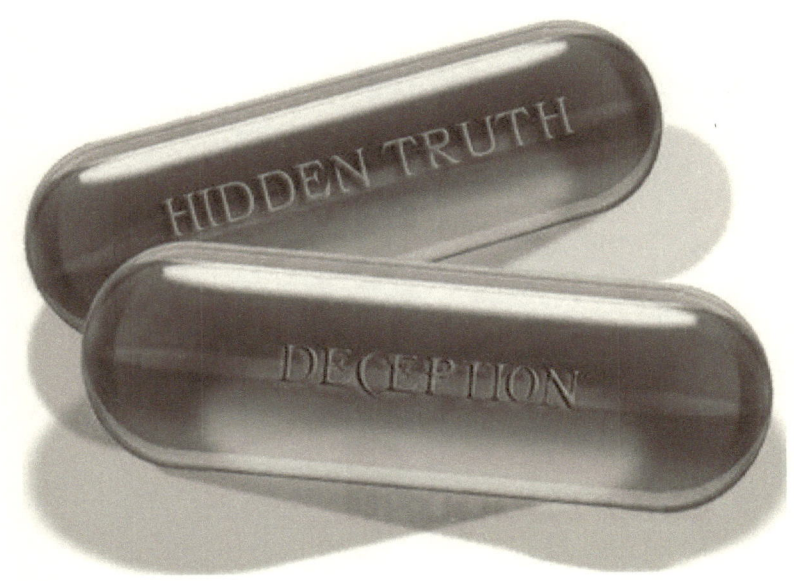

This book is dedicated to my wife, and kids. They are a gift from God and for without him and them I would be nothing. I live for all of them everyday. They drive me to do things I never thought possible.

I also want to dedicate this to the Patriots who each and every day dedicate their lives to waking up the hearts and minds of the American people. You are all the reason I write.

Thank you all very much.

A House with a Broken Foundation

A very famous man once said,

> *"If the American people ever allow private banks to control the issuance of their currencies, first by inflation and then by deflation, the banks and corporations that will grow up around them will deprive the people of all their prosperity until their children will wake up homeless on the continent their fathers conquered."*.

That man was Thomas Jefferson.

Those of you reading this essay will probably find this whole book incredibly ironic as I the author, am a banker by trade.

Yes, that's right an evil banker, I am the living embodiment of what the tea-party and the occupy movement are working to rid the world of, and you know… they are right, banks are bad, the Federal Reserve is bad.

The system is broken and is beyond repair and I am ashamed to say that I have helped to perpetuate the stereo type of the modern banker.

I want to start off first with an analogy for you; imagine if you will a house that it walls have begun to crack.   Would you just plaster over the cracks and hope that it goes away? Plaster will only cover so much before the crack once again takes over and show's its ugliness.

No! You would want to inspect the foundation to make sure that it isn't cracking!

If you can fix the foundation, you shouldn't have to fix the walls anymore.

In order to sway your mindset about the coming financial collapse, I first need to help you inspect the foundation of our banking system. I will do this so you can see from a very real standpoint that will help you to see that it is the foundation that needs to be fixed before the walls can be corrected.

Here is my foundation. I hope that it will help you to understand our bankers and why you and yours need to wake up to the reality of what's coming!

Let's start by understanding how I got here first.

I started my banking career in the year 2000 wide-eyed and ready to take on the world. I started this 12 year journey with Bank of America, where I, like any good peon; I started by answering the telephones.

I worked in a call center where every day millions of small business owners would call in and I would answer their questions about their credit card processing. Some wanted to know where their money went, why they couldn't see it on their statement and most importantly they wanted to know why they were paying so much.

I did my best to always spin their fees in a positive light and to make the bank look good.

I stayed in that position for two years and then found myself yearning for a world where cubicles and a call queue didn't exist.

So I became a personal banker.

I was ready to solve the world's financial problems, and to help people recognize their financial dreams and plan for their futures.

For three years business was good. No, not good, it was great. I opened thousands of accounts, convinced hundreds of families to open up Home Equity Lines of Credit because you never know when, "You will want to buy that new boat or car!"

I was a shylock, a flim-flam man, a loan officer. The checks were rolling in and I was newly married and loved having the extra income. I didn't care where the money came from, as long as it was in my pocket. I decided I wanted more.

So I decided to go into management. I entered Bank of America's management training program and began my upward climb. My wife of one year and I moved from town to town on behalf of BofA and each time the deal got a bit sweeter. I ended up moving closer to home again and found myself the manager of a small rural branch located in Cheney Washington.

I worked at that branch for 8 months and during that time my eyes were opened to the beginning of the struggles people were having.

Cheney only has 2500 residents and half of them are students at the local college. When the college isn't in session, money doesn't flow through the community and many, many people live their lives on State based entitlements and worse yet, manage their bank accounts by how many overdraft fees their welfare or SSI check will cover and yet still allow them to pay their bills. I can't recall how many people I had hour long conversations with who told me virtually the same story.

Their job was seasonal or based on the college and now that the money wasn't there they couldn't pay their bills and I needed to understand and give back the fees that I (the bank) charged.

Time passed, hundreds of conversations went by and I decided to go into business banking instead.

I was tired of listening to the whining of the small town minds and thought that if I went into business banking that I could once again make more money. I took a position of a business specialist for Bank of America and once again I was on the path again to career growth.

I stayed in that role for a year and then moved onto a different bank and then yet another, and on to another. I was constantly looking for the bigger and better opportunity, all the while leaving a wake of financial destruction in my path. I never hesitated to open a credit line for someone who should have never opened it, or recommended someone a product that they really didn't need. I continued to grow in my career eventually became an Assistant Vice President with JPMorgan Chase. I had a team of 23 bankers, I had a territory and most importantly I had money rolling in, and I was finally going to make it big.

It was then the rug was pulled out from underneath me.

I lost my job. My position was "eliminated" and they (being Chase) no longer needed me in my current capacity.

I was offered a position at a fifty percent pay cut.

I took the job because I needed to pay bills and pay for our last child who was about to be born in that following December.
I was panicked.

I didn't know what to do and now I had to tap our savings for my house payment and to pay for fuel in my tank. I began to look for another job ASAP.

I found another one... for a little more money and I moved to yet another bank, another job where I was required to sell products and credit to people who didn't need them.

Now, most people would be bitter about what happened to them, watching their entire career circle the drain and yes, I was for a short time I was very bitter, and sometimes I still feel the bitter burn of anger.

However something happened to me, I discovered something that rocked my world.

I woke up, took the preverbal "red pill" and it changed my world forever.

The Red Pill

Being a huge self confessed nerd one of my favorite movies is the first Matrix movie. There is an amazing scene in the first Matrix movie between Lawrence Fishburn's character Morpheus and Keanu Reeves' character Neo. In that scene Morpheus offers Neo a choice;

> *"You take the blue pill – the story ends, you wake up in your bed and believe whatever you want to believe. You take the red pill – you stay in Wonderland and I show you how deep the rabbit-hole goes."*

Many movie critics and scholars alike have interpreted this "choice" that Neo has to make as this; the blue pill is symbol to remain in blissful ignorance and to remain in the illusion the living world is a good and happy place. Nothing can go wrong. The blue represents fakeness.

The red pill is the embracing of the true and painful reality of what the world truly is.

In the fall of 2011 I took "the red pill" and I woke up to the reality around me.

I can remember the day quite vividly. It was November 23rd the day before Thanksgiving. It was a painfully slow day in banking and I was busy reading up on Bloomberg and surfing the other financial blogs when I ran across a YouTube video and something that startled me.

The video said that our precious Federal Reserve isn't part of our Government, nor is it a Federal agency of any type, it went on to say that the money that You and I use for our everyday expenses is nothing more than paper and backed by virtually nothing and, very soon it is going to be worth nothing.

Those words shocked me. I didn't believe them. "How can this be possible?" I asked myself. "This can't be real...?" I had been a part of this industry for now 12 years and I thought I had known mostly everything that needed to be known about my craft.

I had been through the year 2008 in banking. It was a terrible year.

During that time I worked for the now defunct Washington Mutual bank and I spent hours on the phone convincing clients their monies were safe and that there was nothing to worry about because the "Federal Reserve" would protect them and their money.

I was reeling.

I couldn't believe what I was hearing. But the more I listened to the presentation the more I felt a sick feeling in my stomach. The facts were lining up, the dates were lining up.

No, this was not possible!

Our Government would never let this happen! How could they be so foolish and blind?

But it was true. I decided to begin researching it myself. I had taken "the red pill" of truth and proceeded further down the rabbit hole.

Now at this point you have already written me off as crazy.

Your saying, "You believed a YouTube video? What are you insane? What kind of Wacko are you? Don't you realize the crap out there?"

Your right, it sounds absolutely insane! But then again what did people think of Henry Ford when he told them the idea for the Automobile? Or maybe Bell when he told them that he had a box you could speak into and someone far away could hear you or better yet Tesla when he said he could move electricity without wires!

How about this?

Let me ask you a question;

What do you know about your Government and the financial system?

If someone who knew nothing about the banking system in America came up to you and asked how it worked... could you give them a rudimentary explanation? Could you tell them how the Federal Reserve works?

No?

And why did what I just say earlier in this chapter make you think that I am loony? You don't even know how our banking system works!

What you are now feeling is perfectly valid. I just told you that the system that you have put your hard earned pennies and dollars and your retirement into is broken and your money will soon be worthless. It should make you mad, it should bother you and keep you up at night and mostly it should leave you heavily questioning to what is truly happening in our financial system.

What you have to understand is that you are starting to wake up. You are slowly starting to stir and realizing that what you are hearing is either a really bad nightmare or the truth and all you want to do is go back to sleep. Pinch yourself… go ahead do it. Did you wake up? Or are you still stirring in your preverbal "slumber"?

The financial system is broken, and unfortunately we live in an era where we **cannot** ignore it any longer. We **cannot** allow our children to inherit our problem. There will not be a future for them.

It's time for change, and I am going to help inspire you to make the change and to influence those around you to make the same change too.

The Federal Reserve **must be eliminated**, and our Nation must return to the basics of a constitutional government and a system of a gold and silver based currency.

In the following chapters I'm going to lay out the following truths to support my vision;

- **The Federal Reserve System is system of fraud and lies.**
- **The Federal Government is not your ally. They are trying to keep you dependent and they will control you through your dependency.**

- **The Federal Reserve Act of 1913 needs to be revoked because it is broken and will destroy our financial system even further.**
- **We need to return to a Gold / Silver based currency and why.**
- **What will be the long term consequences if we don't fix the broken system.**
- **How you should prepare your family for the future if we don't fix the system.**
- **Finally what we as citizens need to do - rise up and act and act now or we will fall down and never be able to rise again!**

I want you to prepare yourself. Don't close off your mind.

The information that is going to be given to you is the stuff that movies are made into.

It is radical. It will stretch you.

It is inflammatory and most importantly it is so crucial that you "take the red pill" and wake up to the world around you and begin to realize that we cannot sustain our current way of life for so many reasons.

Take the red pill now and come with me down the preverbal rabbit hole and we'll discover together how deep it goes and how together we can survive this mess we have gotten into.

Living a Lie

Truth # 1 -   The Federal Reserve System is system of fraud and lies.

"It is well that the people of the nation do not understand our banking and monetary system, for if they did, I believe there would be a revolution before tomorrow morning."

Henry Ford

Ford was a visionary and knew that knowledge is power.
As people begin to wake up to what is going on around them they will scream for revolution and change.

Can you imagine it?

You wake up one morning to hear millions of people have descended on their offices of their senators and congress people and demanded change?

The "Occupy" movement of 2011 had a little of this fire. But they didn't know what they were fired up about; they have no clue and still don't know.

They want to "fight the corporate power."

It is commonly known that to put out a fire, you have to douse the flames at the base not pour water of the upper part of the fire.

Attack it at the source so it doesn't flame up again.

Occupy is nothing more than a group of bratty spoiled kids who have squirt guns trying to put out a 3 alarm fire.

But we the "awakened" know what we are fighting for, the abolishment of the Federal Reserve Bank and corrupt financial polices of big government.

We, the awake know what has to change, and you soon will too.

Here is where it all begins, here is where you begin your journey into understanding that the financial system that you and I have believed in for so long is worthless and broken and will be our undoing as a nation.

In order to help you rebuild your foundation and understanding of the lies and manipulation of our nation's money, you must first see the time line for how we as a nation got into this horrible mess.

To start to understand that this system we are currently living in today you have to understand that the idea of a central bank was envisioned more than 239 years ago.

During the year of 1773 the world's richest man Amschel Mayer Rothschild said the following;

"Give me control of a nations money and I care not who makes the laws." That attitude continued to perpetuate down through history and family lines when in 1815 Nathan Rothschild, Amschel's son said;

"I care not what puppet is placed on the throne of England to rule the empire...I know that the man who controls Britain's money supply controls the British Empire. And I control the money supply."

Disturbing huh? But this mindset is what got us started down this misguided road. It is to be noted and understood that the Rothschild's were and still are one of the world's most wealthy families.

They still control an incredible size of the world's wealth and most certainly continue to pull the strings of our economy today. Though their holdings may have changed through the years, they are still heavily invested in bank stocks and wealth manipulation schemes.

On to the beginning of the deception;

We as a nation saw our first bank central founded in 1782 when the Bank of North America was founded and managed by a man named Robert Morris.

People claim that Morris was a visionary, but it only took 16 years for Morris to become fully corrupted. He was jailed in 1798 when he failed to pay his debtors.

Due to the fact that Mr. Morris had friends in high places in congress at that time, they passed what came to be known as the Temporary Bankruptcy Act of 1800. This allowed Mr. Morris to escape debtor's prison and was able to escape with what is come to be known as the first "Golden Parachute".

When the Bank of North America applied for its next charter renewal in 1811, it was voted down and what followed was the war of 1812. This is a war financed by Rothschild families banks and the Bank of England in an effort to draw the newly born America into heavy debt and bankrupt them to force America's hand to reinstate the First Bank of North America, and possibly back under the reign of England.

At this time America didn't have sufficient tax revenue due to the low population to fund the war and things looked very bleak. The war lasted three years and ended in 1815.

In 1816 congress voted to implement the Second Bank of North America which became heavily invested in and financed by the Rothschild family and its holdings. The Bank was given a charter of 20 years.

In 1832 the bank re-applied for their charter and Andrew Jackson being the sitting president (1829 – 1837), veto's its renewal.

Jackson who ran for re-election in 1832 with the slogan of, "Jackson and No-Bank" won his re-election and also strong public support for his cause. Jackson wanted to move the money back to the people and not in the hands of those who are corrupted by it.

At this time a man named Nicholas Biddle was the second president of the Bank of the United States and was very concerned that Jackson had won re-election and was anti-central bank.

In 1833 Jackson began removing the Governments deposits from the Rothschild's central banking system.

Then in 1835, a man named Richard Lawrence attempts to assassinate Andrew Jackson. The gun jams and Jackson is saved by accident. At his trial Richard Lawrence is found not guilty by reason of insanity and claims that very powerful "Banking Interests" hired him to do the job.

Jackson being quite angry about this comes out and says he believes that the Rothschild's were behind the attempt on his life.

In 1836 the Bank Charter expires and the Second Bank of the United States is disbanded and small institutions are chartered and started.

What follows next is the election of Abraham Lincoln and the start of the civil war. Faced with very a limited income from a small tax base and a war on his hands, Lincoln decides after 70 years of using Gold and Silver coin as the currency as was required by the constitution, to break faith with the founding document and print "bank demand notes" rather than borrowing money from the Rothschild's and the other banks.

Not only did Lincoln have demand notes printed. He also had "Legal Tender" notes printed as well. This fact should be noted that Lincoln did his best to back the currency by Gold and Silver however toward the end of his life when the 1863 National Banking Act was passed Lincoln spoke out against the charter and said the following on November 11, 1864;

> *"I see in the near future crisis approaching. It unnerves me and causes me to tremble for the safety of my country. The money power preys upon the nation in times of peace and conspires against in time of adversity.*
>
> *It is more despotic than monarchy, more insolent than autocracy, more selfish than bureaucracy. It denounces, as public enemies, all who questions it method or throws light upon its crimes.*
>
> *I have two great enemies, the Southern Army in front of me and the financial institutions at the rear; the latter is my greatest foe.*
>
> *Corporations have been enthroned and an era of corruption in the high places will follow, and the money power of the country will endeavor to prolong its reign by working upon the prejudices of the people until the wealth is aggregated in the hands of a few and the republic is destroyed."*

Lincoln knew that he had really messed up. He knew that paper currency would ruin America. On April 14th, 1865 Lincoln was killed for his beliefs.

What follows for several decades is the "money power" that Lincoln spoke about and feared running their own agenda for the final implementation of an indefinitely chartered central banking system.

In 1881 the newly appointed President James Garfield had been elected and the charter from the 1863 National Banking Act charter was set to expire. Garfield, being of sound mind and a fiscally conservative man, opposes the renewal and was assassinated by Charles Guiteau, and the vice President Chester A Arthur gives the ok and the "money power" gets its second twenty year charter.

In 1902 that charter was set to expire again. During this time William McKinnly was President and openly opposes the renewal of the charter again. He is assassinated, and Vice President Theodore Roosevelt is named as McKinley's successor.

Here is a very interesting bit of history. Roosevelt belonged to a wealthy banking family and so it was in the best interest of the Central Bank to have Roosevelt in office and positioned as a "progressive" that moves interests moved forward once again and the third charter is approved that was set to expire in 1922.

What follows during the period of 1902 – 1922 is a very interesting election in which the banking interests prove that they once again control the money and the power and we the people don't matter.

In 1912 William Taft was the current president and a popular one at that. Taft then loses his re-election bid by the following political maneuvering; during the election of 1912 Taft had to run against Woodrow Wilson and Teddy Roosevelt.

The party breakdown goes as follows; Taft being the republican, Wilson being the democrat and Roosevelt being from the newly created "bull moose" party which was only formed for this election.

During this election Taft lost the conservative vote due to the votes being split between Roosevelt and Taft, so effectively putting Wilson into office.

Wilson being the winner had absolutely no qualifications for becoming President, except the fact that he was a college professor ran on the premise that he believed that men like JP Morgan should be running the central bank and the country.

With Taft out of the way this paves the road for the newly penned 1913 Federal Reserve act. It took over a hundred years of maneuvering and lies and murder for the bankers to get their way.

Flash forward in time 50 years.

During the period before John F Kennedy's Presidency, no President had ever opposed the Federal Reserve and central banking system.

On June 4th 1963 President Kennedy signed Executive Order 11110.

When President Kennedy signed this Order, it returned to the Federal Government, specifically the Treasury Department, the Constitutional power to create and issue currency money without going through the privately owned Federal Reserve Bank.

President Kennedy's Executive Order 11110 gave the Treasury Department the explicit authority: "to issue silver certificates against any silver bullion, silver, or standard silver dollars in the Treasury."

This means that for every ounce of silver in the U.S. Treasury's vault, the government could introduce new money into circulation based on the silver bullion <u>physically held there</u>.

As a result, more than $4 billion in United States Notes were brought into circulation. They started with $2 and $5 denominations.

$10 and $20 United States Notes were never circulated but were being printed by the Treasury Department when Kennedy was assassinated.

It appears obvious that President Kennedy knew the Federal Reserve Notes being used as the purported legal currency were contrary to the Constitution of the United States of America.

"United States Notes" were issued as an interest-free and debt-free currency backed by silver reserves in the U.S. Treasury. We compared a "Federal Reserve Note" issued from the private central bank of the United States (the Federal Reserve Bank a/k/a Federal Reserve System), with a "United States Note" from the U.S. Treasury issued by President Kennedy's Executive Order.

They almost look alike, except one says "Federal Reserve Note" on the top while the other says "United States Note". Also, the Federal Reserve Note has a green seal and serial number while the United States Note has a red seal and serial number. See the attached photos;

The United States Notes

The Federal Reserve Note

President Kennedy was assassinated on November 22, 1963 and the United States Notes he had issued <u>were immediately</u> taken out of circulation. The deception continued and Federal Reserve Notes once again continued to serve as the currency of the nation.

Kennedy knew that if the silver-backed United States Notes were widely circulated, they would have eliminated the demand for Federal Reserve Notes.

This is a very simple matter of economics. Two currencies cannot compete in the same country if one is sound and the other isn't.

The USN (United States Note) was backed by silver and the FRN (Federal Reserve Note) was not backed by anything of intrinsic value.

Executive Order 11110 should have prevented the national debt from reaching its current level. If LBJ or any subsequent President were to enforce it, it would have almost immediately given the U.S. Government the ability to repay its debt without going to the private Federal Reserve Banks and being charged interest to create new "money".

Yes, that is right, our Government has to pay interest on its own money.

Paper money had been created and men, honest men who believed they were doing the right thing for the nation were killed because the money had corrupted the system and our nation had now been changed forever.

They now thought they could never be stopped.

The foundation for our current financial system is built upon lies and heavy deception. They don't teach you this in school, why would they?

They, the "money power" don't want people educated about their dark past. They want you to think that your money is safe and secure and it will always be there.

If your teacher taught you that our current financial system was built and that men had been killed and lies had been told to the American people about the safety of their money, what would this country do to its self? It would tear itself apart in a matter of days.

People would rush to their currency dealers to buy gold and silver only to be found that it is so far out of their price range. They would then rush to the grocery stores to buy food only to find that their money is no good because and only people with hard currency will be able to purchase goods and services at a severely inflated rate.

People will starve, family's will die, society as we know it will tear itself apart and it will be on the heads of our politicians and people who know the checkered history and could have done something about it.

Guess what? Where will they be when it collapses?

They will be nowhere to be found when it all falls apart.

They will be busy trying to save themselves and their families not yours.

The Permanent Crutch

Truth # 2 - **The Federal Government is not your ally. They are trying to keep you dependent and they will control you through your dependency.**

"Freedom is not empowerment. Empowerment is what the Serbs have in Bosnia. Anybody can grab a gun and be empowered. It's not entitlement. An entitlement is what people on welfare get, and how free are they? It's not an endlessly expanding list of rights -- the "right" to education, the "right" to health care, the "right" to food and housing.

That's not freedom, that's dependency. Those aren't rights; those are rations of slavery -- hay and a barn for human cattle. There's only one basic human right, the right to do as you damn well please. And with it comes the only basic human duty, the duty to take the consequences."

PJ O'Rourke

In early 2012 a young women named Amanda Clayton won the lottery in Lincoln Park Michigan. Why is this important?

Because after she won the lottery she still collected and used food stamps until someone had the good conscience enough and turn her in to CNN.

CNN decided to confront her with her flagrant fraud. Then when asked why she was abusing her states entitlement program, she said the following,

> *"I thought that they would cut me off, but since they didn't I thought maybe it was OK because I'm not working and I feel that it's OK because I have no income, and I have bills to pay. I have two houses."*

Yes, that's right two houses. She has two houses! If as a tax-paying American that doesn't get your blood boiling well… you're probably dead or Canadian. Just kidding, we love our brothers and sisters to the north!

This blatant fraud has happened before too! In May of 2011 a Michigan man won 2 million dollars in the lottery and stayed on food stamps. He unlike the other young women called the state to let them know that he had won. Yet they continued to give him food stamps.

Even after the state went after him for the money for the food stamps abuse he recounted,

> *"If you're going to try to make me feel bad, you aren't going to do it!"*

What we are seeing here in these two examples is what is happening all over this nation. The flagrant abuse of the welfare entitlement system, but more importantly, the reliance on the system permanently as a lifestyle.

Our Government is intentionally keeping Americans poor. They will tell you they aren't, but too many facts point to the fact that it is easy to control people through the system when you control the goods and services they consume.

Here are some very disturbing statistics according to an April 13th 2011 news filling by CNN;

> **1 in 6 Americans get help from the Government, that working out to roughly 14% or 43,622,868 people!**

> **In June 1 in 6 people are on Medicaid / Medicare with more than 50 Million people registering in 2010 alone!**

> **In January 2011 more than 44.2 Million people were on food stamps. That is up by 4.7 million in the previous year.**

> **More than 8.3 million people are collecting unemployment benefits, while that number is down from the previous year where 12 million filed. It is still double the amount of people who filed in 2007. Currently in America 8.3 million Americans are on unemployment.**

So while people sit at home collecting their unemployment checks they become victims of the system, becoming reliant on it to provide for them, there is no motivation to find a job.

The federal regulation is now a 59 week period to find a job and the average American on unemployment makes three quarters of what they used to make on their full time work.

If you can bare it, you can take a year off to look for work, and we the tax payers are paying for it!

Since 2010 unemployment benefits have been extended three times to accommodate Americans who can't find jobs they like.

Not that there aren't jobs available, there just isn't available jobs that they find ideal. American has become lazy, slow and has fallen behind the world in many, many different categories.

According the March 13th 2012 Bureau of Labor and Statics press release there were 3.5 million job openings in January 2012, yet only 227,000 people were hired that month. So what is the problem?

Here is the simple answer. Welfare pays better. Much better!

Let's see what the breakdown works out to be; for an average family of four in Washington State (DHS.WA.GOV) you can get the following social entitlements;

➢ **Welfare (food stamps)for your groceries ($668)**

➢ **TANF cash for your expenses ($200)**

➢ **HUD to pay your rent ($800 - 900)**

➢ **S.N.A.P to pay for your utilities ($225 average)**

➢ **SSI ($1300 for individuals) for extra pocket money if you can get a note from your doctor and are "clinically depressed".**

➢ **Medicare for your health and free dental (between $1000 - 2000 per family depending on amount of care you receive each month.)**

Wow. Sounds like a pretty sweet deal huh?

In fact if you were an average family of four you could make $4,193 dollars per month just in government benefits per month that is $50,316.00 per year! So if 1 in 6 (43,622,868) Americans are on these services that is an astounding estimated **$2,194,928,226,288.00** per month on the average!

That is just obscene.

Now, I am not saying we need to cut off all social service programs.

But when those types of dollar figures are on the table there we will we have to establish that there are many Americans who truly do need it, but a larger majority who don't.

But, it is so easy to get on and stay on benefits and our Government makes it easy to "live" within the system because the government wants it and makes it easy. That is an extremely dangerous way to live, hand to mouth and dependent on a government whose money system as you have read is built on murder and lies. They leverage the debt. They need you to spend their money. As long as you spend their money, you need them, <u>and they own you</u>.

We are dependent on them; they know that if we continue to live on their terms, they can dictate whatever they want to us through those terms.

Which leads me to this, now that we are a dependent on the Government for everything, our food, homes and healthcare what will our Government do? How will that change our lives? How will they begin to dictate what you can and cannot do?

Here is how they will start to do it.

On March 16th 2012 President Obama signed executive order to update the "National Defense Resource Preparedness" plan. This order effectively updates the original order, 12919 originally signed in June of 1994. This order also accompanies the bill signed on New Year's Eve 2011 also known as the NDAA, or National Defense Authorization Act.

There are several items in this plan that are very concerning to me as well as they should be to you. Now that a larger portion of the American Economy is dependent on the government for sustenance; your President with his word can under section 308 of the new executive order can;

(a)   Procure and install additional equipment, facilities, processes, or improvements to plants, factories, and other industrial facilities owned by the Federal Government and to procure and install Government owned equipment in plants, factories, or other industrial facilities **<u>owned by private persons</u>**.

So in plain english, the Military and Government can take your personal property, throw it away or destroy it and then install their own computers, monitoring equipment, internet connection, manufacturing equipment, tanks, guns, and troops on your personal property, or your business property.

They can now also under section 102;

> (c) be prepared, in the event of a potential threat to the security of the United States, to take actions necessary to ensure the **availability of adequate resources and production capability, including services and critical technology, for national defense requirements.**

That should scare the pants off of you.

The Government just said in law that they could take whatever they want from you to ensure for national defense. You thought you had guns, guess what, they are gone! They will say, "We need them for our national defense". You thought you were putting food storage aside for your family, guess what they will say too; "our Government needs that Sir / Madam. I'm sorry but our troops need it more than you!"

This is also known as the "re-distribution" of wealth a popular concept under communism.

Your supplies, homes, computers, guns, ammunition and medical supplies have now become the property of the United States Government. Welcome to Communism!

Guess who else did this in a time of war? The Nazi's! They used the hair, clothing and "resources" of the Jewish people to help their war machine. You know who else did it too? The Russians under Joseph Stalin!

There are some very wordy portions of this order, but the scariest part of this executive order that should absolutely cause you to fall out of your chair is that all of this can be enacted in peace-time.

Section 102 Paragraph B and C say;

> (b) assess on an ongoing basis the capability of the domestic industrial and technological base to satisfy requirements in **peacetime** and times of national emergency, specifically evaluating the availability of the most critical resource and production sources, including subcontractors and suppliers, materials, skilled labor, and professional and technical personnel;

> (c) be prepared, in the event of a **potential threat** to the security of the United States, to take actions necessary to ensure the availability of adequate resources and production capability, including services and critical technology, for national defense requirements;

So now you can see that in peacetime or war time the President can enact this order. Even when a potential threat is minimal they / he can implement these set of strict laws, or in other words implement martial law when they feel like it.

There are also additional parts of this executive order that discuss "personnel" and it speaks of the ability to move "resources" or people and families to where they need them and want them.

So what does this mean to all of us?

When you give away your freedoms through the acceptance of government entitlements they can tell you where to go, when and how much to eat and drink, when to sleep and how you have to work for them now to get your entitlement.

They own you!

They control you through the entitlement, they will cause you to do things for your entitlement that you don't want to do. You will someday have to make really horrible choices.

Now is the time work to get away from your entitlement so you can gain your freedom back! Stop the control and begin think for yourself.

Light the Torches

Truth # 3 - The Federal Reserve Act of 1913 needs to be revoked because it is broken and will destroy our system even further.

"We have, in this country, one of the most corrupt institutions the world has ever known. I refer to the Federal Reserve Board. This evil institution has impoverished the people of the United States and has practically bankrupted our government. It has done this through the corrupt practices of the moneyed vultures who control it".

> — Congressman Louis T. McFadden in 1932 (Rep. Pa)

Bonds, Quantitative Easing, credit default swaps, Fractional Reserve Banking. All are very fancy terms and sometimes quoted to be massively confusing to the American listener. It's what the money power wants you to feel when you think about the Fed and its role in the American Economy.

I want to help you to find your way through the mire of the terminology and understand what the role of the Fed is and how it is incredibly bad for the future of our country.

I don't want you to feel that what one person told me in my research for my book, *"There are other smarter people than I who control things... I really don't know how the whole thing works..."*

So, to help you understand the necessity of why the Federal Reserve needs to be removed, we have to understand what powers they have and why.

When the Federal Reserve Act of 1913 was written, the law makers who did it thought they had their best in mind. They knew that we couldn't sustain our current spending. They didn't care about us.

The Federal Reserve knows the end is coming. The current chairman has stated it on multiple occasions. They have tired to fix it multiple times. They can't. They are out of options.

That is why the money power needs to maintain control.

They know our tax base will never cover our expenses.

They know they make a killing off of the interest we as a nation would pay and pay and we will never even make a dent in the principal.

What they didn't count on was the fact that they couldn't sustain our level of borrowing requests and they (the Fed) had to go to the rest of the world to find money.

They thought that if they could control the way that the money flowed through the economy that they could make lots of money for themselves by making our currency the most powerful in the world.

They can't stop the machine. Once they stop it, it will never begin again.

So in the spirit of, *"know the enemy"*:

Here is how the Federal Reserve is made up;

The Chairmen of the Federal Reserve is currently Ben Bernanke, he is the mouth piece of the board. He is appointed by the President of the United States.

Below him is a Board of Governors who make the decisions for the Fed. Due to the fact that the Fed is a NGA or "non-government agency" the President of the United States, Congress or the Senate has no say over how the decisions are made or why they are made in the first place.

The ironic fact in this is that our President also appoints the people to the board, but since the board cannot be "influenced" by partisan politics they can't be "connected" to our Government.

Below the Board is the 12 Corporate Banks that own and control the Federal Reserve. Yes, private banks who own stock in the Fed control our money. Not our Government established by the people. Private for-profit money controls the flow of money in the economy.

Finally the level below them is are the FDIC member banks that you and I bank with everyday. (See illustration).

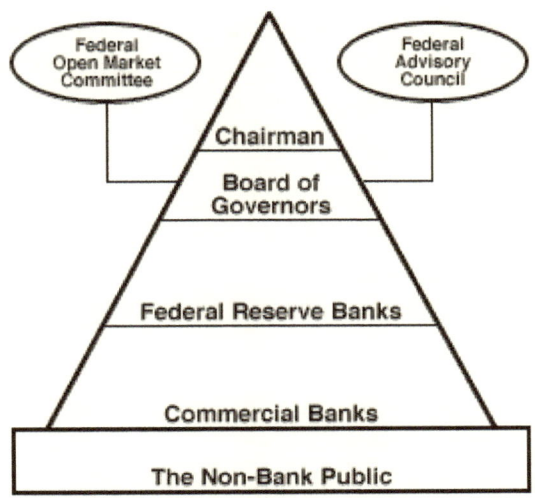

So how does money get into the economy? Well the first step is that someone has to need it.

So let's say you wanted a get a loan for a shiny new car. You don't have the money right? But guess who does? "PJ Gorman" bank!

So you march on down to the bank and say to your favorite banker, "Mr. Banker, I would like a new car, can you loan me $45,000.00?"

Your banker responds, "For you Mr. or Mrs. Customer, anything!" One tiny little problem, they don't actually have the money in the vault to loan you.

Now ... since the bank really doesn't have that money you need, they call the Federal Reserve and tell them they need money to back the loan they sold.

So the Federal Reserve fires up the printing presses and off the money goes to PJ Gorman Bank to fund the loan you just took out.

Wait... wait just a second. Did you just say fire up the presses?

Yes, yes I just did.

The Fed just prints the money the bank wants, loans it to them at a cost, and into the economy it goes. They "wire" it to the banks accounts and it magically appears for the banks to spend.

Now you're saying, "Well... where does the money come from to secure the money they just printed?"

Well they come from the Fed raising and lowering the prime interest rate. They also sell bonds to other countries to with a promise to repay them someday for they money that was loaned to them.

Its that simple.

But there is a big, big problem here.

There is nothing, <u>absolutely nothing in our constitution that says that this is ok</u>. In fact it is outright illegal according to our constitution. Here is what the 10th Amendment says about currency;

"No State shall enter into any Treaty, Alliance, or Confederation; grant Letters of Marque and Reprisal; coin Money;emit Bills of Credit; <u>make any thing but gold and silver Coin a Tender in Payment of Debts</u>; pass any Bill of Attainder, ex post facto Law, or Law impairing the Obligation of Contracts, or grant any Title of Nobility."

These are the words of our fore-fathers. The founders, the architects of our once great nation. They knew that paper currency was a bad thing. Here is what George Washington had to say about it;

"But if in the pursuit of the means we should unfortunately stumble again on unfunded paper money or any similar species of fraud, we shall assuredly give a fatal stab to our national credit in its infancy. Paper money will invariably operate in the body of politics as spirit liquors on the human body. They prey on the vitals and ultimately destroy them."

He could see it... our founding fathers could see it. Why can't we? Why can't they?

But there are more questions; if we are only supposed to use Gold and Silver... don't we have enough to cover our current currency?

Short Answer; No.

We have no Gold or Silver to cover our current money. Your bank may say "FDIC Insured" but that guarantee is worthless, there isn't an ounce of gold to back the currency.

Guess what? I have a very shocking statement for you.

Fort Knox is empty.

There is not enough Gold or Silver to back your retirement, and most importantly your checking account that you want to buy groceries and fuel with later today. Disturbing? Yes... let me add some clarification for you.

Here is a bit of history to bring you up to date on why our currency is worthless at the moment.

Here is the short version.

In 1971 when Richard Nixon was President and We (The US) were still a part of the Brett Bretton Woods system of international financial exchange established toward the end of WWII.

This system allowed anyone who held the currency of the United States to convert it and withdrawal it in gold. They could export it out of the country and import it to their country at their own security risk.

By the early 1970's the US was really racking up quite the bill for the Vietnam war and for the first time in the 20th Century we were having trouble paying the piper for our activities. The world sat up and began to take notice that we were beginning to default and so they came a-knocking. During the first six months of 1971 over $22 billion dollars in gold left our countries vaults.

Then later that year after Germany decided to leave the Bretton Woods system after the US dollar was beginning to fall in value in comparison to Germany's mark and the rest of Europe's currencies.

France and Switzerland followed Germany's example and together pulled almost $191 million in Gold reserves as well. Nixon and team had to do something. So they passed a 90-day wage and price freeze, a 10 percent import surcharge, and, most importantly, "closed the gold conversion window", ending convertibility between US dollars and gold. The President and his fifteen advisers made that decision without consulting the members of the international monetary system, so the international community informally named it the "Nixon shock".

Given the importance of the announcement and its impact upon foreign currencies presidential advisers recalled that they spent more time deciding when to publicly announce the controversial plan than they spent creating the plan.

So what did the Fed do after this point? They started borrowing from other countries in the form of selling bonds. They needed the money to fund the operations of the Army the Government and the beginning to retire social security recipients. In fact as the soldiers returned from war thus began the exit of another generation from America's work force. So the Fed began to sell more long term bonds.

The young men returning home needed jobs and many of the people who had worked through WWII were now wanting to retire and enjoy life in the now war-less USA.

But a bigger problem was brewing. Our tax base was beginning to shrink due to returning un-employed vets.

Due to the past inflation from the gold conversion crisis unemployment went up, and people didn't have money or didn't earn it so the tax base shrank and the US couldn't pay the Fed back for the money it was borrowing.

But the money power missed something. They didn't replace the gold! They went completely in the opposite direction of what we should have done. The Fed thought that the mess had blown over now that Nixon had stopped the World from taking our gold that used to back our currency.

The Fed didn't plan ahead. They have been thinking like a horny teenager with a credit card and hot girlfriend. When the money runs out, she is going to leave, the relationship will fall apart!

The Fed is lending out money they don't have. People are cashing in their government bonds at record rates and more and more people apply for Government benefits and social security every day!

How can we make money out of thin air and expect that it will not eventually catch up with us?

The world knows it, and they are getting ready to do something about it and it will change our lives forever as we know it! Here is the brutal truth; The Fed doesn't care about you! You are just a number and dollar symbol on a lousy piece of paper to them.

They have a business to run and a debt to manage; they have to stave off the economic collapse as long as they can, and they know that time is running out.

When we don't have the money to pay the bills anymore, very soon that the system will implode on itself.

The rest of the world knows this. We have to repeal the Federal Reserve act of 1913, and return to the gold or silver standard to back our currency.

They (the world) started buying up gold and silver from other sources, even our own American Corporations! Now in 2012 we are in a real danger of having the bottom fall out from underneath us, and here is how it is going to happen.

Adapt or Die

Truth # 4 -   We need to return to a Gold / Silver based currency and why.

Gold. It's all about the Gold.

In late 2012 the Peoples Republic of China is targeted to launch what will be known as "PAGE" or the "Pan American Gold Exchange". Why would they launch it you say? Well this is why.

Right now the World Gold Exchanges are controlled in both London and America, yes America... We still have some gold left, but mostly it isn't ours.

We just housing it, we don't own it.

China has been buying up records amounts of gold in the past 10 years and importing it to China. In fact, in 2012 China surpassed the country of India in its demand for physical gold. How have they been able to afford that you ask?

Well it's simple. China has been loaning us unreal amounts of money over the past 15 plus years to help us pay our debts and fund our governmental operations.

China owns a significant portion of our debt. Remember the debt clock at the 2012 Republican National Convention?

Well... a better portion of that debt is owned to China!

The interest we have been paying to them has helped them to fund their purchase of serious gold and gold based assets like American gold and silver mines as well as raw gold too.

Yes, they are using our own money and our natural resources against us.

We have been paying them back by having the Fed print more "dollars" but we are just skimming the surface by just paying the interest and not of the principal of our line of credit with China.

In fact the Chinese government has gone as far as to allow their citizens to begin owning their own gold again and using it as a currency too. They still use the Yuan, but the Chinese government has set up shops all over China that allows their citizens to buy gold and silver bars to keep for themselves.

So when China launches PAGE, the rest of the world will have another source to buy Gold from rather from the Americans and the British. China may even go as far as to say they will not do any business with any country that doesn't have a currency backed by gold because the money is no good.

We as a nation will attempt to buy gold but when China launches P.A.G.E the price of gold and silver will exponentially increase and we won't even be able to afford it from our friends in London.

So what will we do to counter the rest of the world using gold to back their currency?

Will we have to either illegally steal the gold that is on our soil in a "manifest destiny" style seizure, or steal it from our own people who own gold privately?

Franklin Roosevelt did in 1933 when he signed Executive Order # 6102 forbidding the hoarding of gold, gold coin and loose gold. They even went as far as to make it a criminal act to do so. What else would they do? Close down all the jewelers and size their gold under Executive Order # 12919 that President Obama just updated to preserve "resources"? Or it will leave our country and we will have to buy gold from China and London or wherever else we can get it.

But wait... if our currency is worth nothing, what do we have to pay the world back with? Land? Military? Buildings? Supplies? .... Here is a horrible thought... what if we have to pay using our own people?

Here is the other massive problem.

Based on a June 1st, 2012 news filing by both RT.com and BusinessInsder.com; China, Japan and now South Korea will conduct all their trade between their respective countries in their native currency, not the American dollar. When the dollar, which has been used for decades as the reserve currency of the world stops being used for trade we also lose the trade income too!

When our money becomes worth nothing, what we will we pay for our oil with? What will we pay our tariffs to other countries with?

If we were to go to Saudi Arabia and ask for more oil, they are going to tell us to go away and leave them alone. They won't be able to sell to us because our currency is going to be worth nothing!

Even worse, when our currency fails, it could transform the Yuan, China's currency into the world's reserve currency, which in 2012 the **BRIC** nations (Brazil, Russia, India and China) began using.

Who will do business with a country that has so much red tape that to tap any natural resource? The Chinese have known this have spent years buying up stock in American based gold companies and buying their own mines as well!

You and I know that our bureaucracy in America is pitiful. It always takes a committee, then you have to get back the EPA, and who knows who else and then an only then an act of God to get something accomplished in the United States.

We have nothing left in the vaults!

We need to figure out what to do! If we don't people will starve and die. Our Nation will descend into social chaos.
<u>We have to return to the gold or silver standard</u>! We don't have a choice. Our money is worth nothing and we don't fix as soon as possible. Things will get worse; in fact it will become downright terrible.

Let me paint a picture for you of what will happen if we don't fix this problem.

The Fiscal Cliff

Truth # 5 -   What will be the long term consequences if we don't fix the broken system.

To help you to understand how the economic collapse will look, I am going to paint you a picture of what it will look like during this time period. Now, the events in which I illustrate how it is going to happen maybe won't be exactly on the time line, but it could be close.

I won't lie to you; I am not a psychic or any sort of sooth-sayer. I am just an banker, and I watched what happened in my industry in 2008. But as I paint the picture, I will use my view point and track record of what I experienced to elaborate on it how dire it is going to be.

Hope you're sitting down.

Here we go;

The decline will start off just any other normal day.

It's a Monday.

You woke up around 7:00 and headed for the shower, your wife has one of the morning shows on the T.V in the living room. You over hear it talking about how much fuel prices have risen and what Americans are doing to cope with the rising costs.

You live in a reasonable size city. Your think your city is isolated. Your commute really isn't that long and yes, the prices have been hitting you pretty hard in the pocket book.

That's ok. "We have been tightening our belt and we just don't go out to eat as often," you tell yourself. "We'll make due… we always figure it out."

You're done with your shower and are dressed and you return to the kitchen for some coffee and breakfast. The news is still on the kids are eating cereal.

Your wife looks at you and says…

"The news was just talking about how much the price of gold has been going up, I wonder how much I could fetch for one of the necklaces I've got laying around?"

"Ah, don't worry about it, were just fine…we're making due."
You tell or her.

She follows up with, "Oh… and I need to run to the market today to pick up more diapers for the baby and get stuff for dinner's next week."

"Ok… sounds good, just let me know how much you spend and I'll put it in the checkbook." You respond.

You decide to head to work after that, you kiss your wife and kids and head to your car.

On the way to work you decide to stop for fuel. Ouch! $3.90 per gallon! Geez… when did that go up? It was just $3.65 the other day.

You get to work and your co-worker stops you on the way in, "Hey… you'd better read CNN this morning… big stuff brewing in China…"

"Yeah, sure thing… I'll get right on it…" you smirk and think to yourself, "Why is everyone so hot on the news this morning?"

A couple of hours go by and you find yourself with a few minutes on your hands to you decide to check CNN for the news. The headline reads,

"CHINA ANNOUNCES NO MORE PURCHASES OF US DEBT."

"Hmm…What does that have to do with me…? As long as I have a steady paycheck that's all I care about. What's everyone worried about?"

You pass the day normally and head home that night. As you pass the fuel station by your house the new per gallon price reads, 4.05 per gallon. "Holy crap…what is going on?" There are a few more cars than normal at the station … but it is rush hour after all.

When you get home your spouse has the T.V on again.

They say, "The President came on T.V this evening and told everyone that we are going to have to expect some spending cuts to overcome some budget short falls…but I don't think that will affect us much. You have a good job and were doing fine."

The evening progresses on a normal pace and you head to bed. The next morning you wake up, same routine but this time the news stations are talking about how some Government, Military, Social Security, and entitlement payments and payroll might be delayed this month, but congress is working on a way to get it taken care of.

They are discussing raising the debt ceiling limit and it is a heated debate. The news shows some pictures of some yelling government employees in a protest.

You announce to your family "Ah… they'll fix it, they always figure out some way."

Then the story changes to some reporter discussing the start of something call "P.A.G.E" or the "Pan American Gold Exchange" and how it's making gold very expensive to buy.

The Chinese also announce in this news cast that they are now backing their currency by gold and that their markets are open to the world to buy gold from them.

Finally the news announcer also talks about how since the Chinese have gone off the dollar earlier this year, relations between the United States have been very tense. The T.V flashes images of Asian people holding gold necklaces and rings, then on to images of people outside of the US Embassy holding signs and yelling.

You head to work, on the way you notice the fuel prices again. $5.10! "What in the world? These lousy gas station owners! They are just trying to steal from us with all this economic fear! This is terrible! The Government should really step in and do something about this!" You continue to rant and rave to yourself on the way to work.

You settle in and begin your day and for a while things are back to normal. Your wife calls on the phone, she is done at the grocery store and she is pissed. "I can't believe how expense things were! Milk was $4.15 a gallon. We spent $300 hundred dollars! We never spend three hundred dollars! Geez it was busy in there today!"

Your week continues on and everyday you see things get a bit more expense during each day you head to work. This goes on for the next three weeks, every day you do the same routine, and every day a bit more.

Finally things start to ratchet up.

It is a Thursday afternoon and the President comes on television for an emergency news conference. You and your co-workers go in to the conference room and turn it on. The President comes out. He looks very dismal, and very tired. You think, "Glad I don't have his job..."

He starts off by talking about how the tough times that make us as Americans a tough hearty breed and we have faced tough times a nation before and we have succeeded.

"Yeah, yeah... same old stuff... what is he going to do about it?" Someone says.

Then he says this, "As Americans, our currency has always been a symbol the world could rely on to look to for hope and security, and today it is severely threatened. We are asking you as Americans to take a moment and look into your hearts and should you feel the need donate your gently used gold at any Army Recruiting center. Help your country! Help your friends and family, we as a nation depend on you to help the effort to strengthen and back our economy. You are America!"

He continues on, "In terms of our Military, our Employees and our Seniors, we are going to ask for a little more patience in getting you your money. We are currently working with our Allies through the world to work on strengthening our relationships with them to ensure that doors for trade continue to stay open and the dollar stays as strong."

He ends with, "Good afternoon and May God bless America."
"Yeah right... I'm not going to give them anything!" Your co-worker announces. "They have plenty of "gold" to back things with. They are just being greedy!"

As you walk back to your desk you think, "Well... I guess I'm just going to have to tighten up my finances again and we'll make due."

The day moves on and you head home. That night at the dinner table your spouse looks concerned. "Why do they want our gold?" she asks.

"Don't worry, they have gold... they are just asking for volunteers, nothing more than that...The country will get through this... we always do..."

Just then the door bell rings, you head to the door and open it.

"Hi sir, my name is Sarah Thomson and this is Tony Randall, we are from the Department of Homeland Security, and we are going door to door to ask you as Americans to donate your gently used gold and silver to nation to help with our currency situation. Would you have anything you would like to donate?"

"Um... no thank you not today." You say politely.

"Are you sure? Everyone can do their part! Don't you have something you can give?" she responds back with.

"Not tonight. Have a good night." You say. As you gently close the door she begins to write something on a clip board, you can't make it out... "Probably just some nasty note about me. " you think.

You go back to the table, "Who was that?" you wife asks, "Someone from the Department of Homeland Security are asking for gold and silver donations."

"What?' she says, 'can't they figure this whole mess out? They are the ones who got us into this mess!" she says.

"I agree' you say. 'Let's not worry about it. Pass the potatoes please..."

This goes on for the next three weeks, the first week it was just the one visit from the DHS people, the second week it was two times and the third week it was three times and during the third week they show up at your home with a US soldier.

You tell them this time around that you would appreciate it if they stopped bothering you.

They don't like that answer and the soldier says; "Sir, we have been tasked by the Government to collect as much gold as we can to help everyone, are you sure you can't donate something? How about your wedding ring? You know you're married; can't you donate it to cause?

You have had it. "I'm not giving you my wedding ring, get off my property and leave us alone!"

You begin to close the door, the solider puts his hand on the door. "Sir, you should really consider donating!"

"Take your hand off my door!" you shout. He complies. But he does it begrudgingly.

You close the door and think. "This is so stupid! Can't they just call in some of the debts other countries owe us?"

A few moments later, you hear a scream outside. You re-open up the door and run out on to the front porch. Your neighbor is lying on the ground and the soldier is on top of him hand cuffing him!

"What happened?" you ask his wife.

"Joe got mad and shoved the soldier and told him to get off our property! Then they slammed him to the ground and they are taking him away!"

"Where are you taking him?" she is screaming, you hold her back as she starts crying and trying to grab at her husband. People are starting to come out of their houses to see what is going on.

Just then a military vehicle drives up and several soldiers get out and help to haul Joe into their car, they take off, tires screeching and the two DHS officers in a car behind them.

Your head is spinning. What the hell just happened? How can they do this?

You get Joe's wife calmed down and tell her that he is going to be fine and she will need to call their attorney in the morning. You head home. It's about 8 pm you decide to watch some T.V to take your mind off what just happened.

You turn to CNN.

This was a bad choice.

The story is about some riots that are taking place in some major city in America, and that gangs of people right now are scrambling to get fuel and groceries and on the heels of the President's announcement that this month's welfare payments would not be made and that social security would not be made either.

He also says something about Executive Order # 12919 and beginning to preserving the nation's resources. What the heck is

Executive Order 12919? The T.V then turns to some footage of shelves in a store that appears very empty except for some paper plates and other non important goods.

You turn the TV off. You tell your wife, "I think I'm going to head to the store to pick up a few things. We may want to keep a few staples on hand". She agrees.

You head to your car and as you drive by the fuel station at the house they line is ridiculously long. $5.65 per gallon the sign reads. You let out a heavy sigh. "They're robbing us blind" you say.

You get to the store and find that everyone else in the neighborhood had the same idea. It seems like the whole city is here! People are everywhere. Shopping carts packed with canned goods!

You grab a cart and manage to get to the canned goods isle. You start grabbing what you can, 5 cans of fruit, 4 cans of beans, spam, chicken, whatever you can get your hands on you put it in your cart. This continues on until your cart is full. You look around. There are shelves empty everywhere!

You are finally ready to check out. You get to the front of the line. The checker and bagger looked stressed out and the checker rudely says, "You'll have to pay in cash, the debit and credit cards don't seem to be working tonight."

Thankfully, you have enough cash in your wallet to pay for the groceries. On your way out you hear two men start to fight. They are screaming about the last can of beans and then they start throwing punches! People gather around to watch the fight and you sneak out to your car and get home fast.

You unload your groceries when you get a call from your boss on the phone.

"Hey ... don't worry about coming in tomorrow. The power is out down here and supposedly they are sending someone out to repair it tomorrow. They say that someone tried to steal the copper out of the substation. Just take the day off ... you have the vacation time anyway!"

"Ok ... sounds good! Thanks." You quietly hang up the phone. Hey...not bad, a day off.

The next morning the President is on the TV again. This time he is saying that he activated the National Guard and is declaring a national emergency and they will be going house to house to look for additional gold or silver to back the currency situation and that per Executive Order # 6102 we will have to give them what we have.

He continues on, that "we as Americans have to recognize that we have to sacrifice and preserve our resources!"

He finishes that if we don't give what we can we could face possible imprisonment and that we all need to help.

"What the hell??" You yell at the T.V, "This is bullshit! They can't take our stuff from us!"

Your spouse comes in the room and tells you to calm down, "Quiet! The kids can hear you...they canceled school today too; I heard it on the radio today, something about having limited resources and the teachers pay. They said they were looking at a three day school week. But it's canceled for the remainder of the week while they figure a new educational plan."

"Geez... What the heck is going on?" You tell your wife to keep the kids in doors today;

"I'm going to make some phone calls to find out what is going on."

You go to pick up your phone. No dial tone. You grab your cell phone. You manage to get through to your boss after 10 tries. He sounds out of breath.

"They are rioting here downtown! People are everywhere! And they're pissed! They have broken out the front windows on our building and are looking for stuff to steal. I have been here since 5:30 this morning when the alarm went off this morning. Don't ...co...wn....ere!..... Gotta go! They're in the building....! "

Click. The line goes dead. You feel the sweat starting to build.

You try calling your parents, both of them are retired and live in Arizona and live on social security. There is no answer on their phone.

Your worried, seriously worried. You try and try, but you can never get through. "Crap...This is really, really bad..." you can't help yourself. You're really worried now.

A couple of hours go by and you hear a loud speaker outside, it's the military.

"Attention Citizens! Attention Citizens! This is a public announcement! Starting today, the Government requests that you bring all items of value, gold, silver, coins, household items that contain precious metals and your firearms to the collection truck now please. If you do not present your items, our teams will go house to house and search for these needed items....'

They continue on;

'Per Presidential order if you are found in possession of these items after today, it will be an offense punishable by imprisonment and seizure of your personal assets!

We are also announcing a curfew effective sundown each day! If you are caught out of doors after sundown you will be detained and questioned and your personal assets may be potentially taken for the good of the country."

"Imprisonment? You have got to be kidding!" you think.
You decide that you do not want to attract any unwanted attention to yourself and your family. You run up stairs and find some cheap jewelry and tell your wife to hide the rest. You don't want the soldiers in your home so you go out and get in line.

You then hear your neighbor down the block yell… "The hell you're taking my stuff!" A shot rings out! A soldier is down!

You hit the ground just as you hear the other your other neighbors start to yell. You hear more gunfire.

You run back to your house, lock the door behind you and take a deep breath. You tell your family to head for the basement while sounds of people shouting and gun fire continue upstairs through the night. The kids are really scared and the baby won't stop crying.

"Oh God… what is happening?

When you come up the next morning you find that your front windows are broken and glass is everywhere. There is a rock on the floor on the baby's favorite play mat. Your wife breaks into a sob, the kids she crying and start to cry again.

You are in shock and walk outside.

The DHS trucks are all through the neighborhood and are arresting your neighbors who shot at them. You go outside and watch them being lead him away to a military vehicle.

Men in handcuffs are fighting their captors and screaming, women and children are all crying too. Everyone is going.

Your kids cry when they see their friends loaded into the big trucks. The soldiers are carrying your neighbor's belongings and loading them on another truck.

"Where are you taking them?" You yell to a soldier.

"We're taking them to a DHS relocation and re-education facility, if you want to join them keep talking!"

You quiet down and head next store ask Joe's wife if her lawyer has heard from him. She says that last she heard from her lawyer, they took him to a "Department of Homeland Security detention center" and that she would hear from him soon. But she never does.

When will this stop? Are we next? What will I do for my family?

Take a breath. Is your heart racing yet? Are you slightly panicked? Good you should be!

Congratulations.

You are now living under Martial Law and at the mercy of the Government.

If I were to keep going with the story you would eventually see the man in the story run out of food for his family and begin to trade away his belongings for food.

The Government would eventually step in to give some rations to the people but it would never be enough to last him and his family. He would lose everything, his home, his food, his guns, and most importantly his constitutional freedoms.

His family like millions of others will probably starve and die.

Maybe they will survive; maybe they will leave and find a place they can re-establish. Maybe civil war breaks out.

Maybe the country is salvaged.

But did you observe how it happened? Slowly, over a period of weeks, not all right away. Civil unrest didn't happen right away. It wasn't the stuff movies are made from. It was a slow decent off the fiscal cliff.

But once it began, there was no stopping it.

I didn't even go into what would happen to the banks or the stock markets in this circumstance.

It is a very sad fact that millions of people who didn't plan ahead or wake up to what was going on around them will starve and die.

This has happened before in history. It happened to the Soviets; it happened in the Balkins, it happened in Rome, and currently is it getting ready to happen in Greece, Spain and Italy... and we'll be next.

People don't learn from history.

Why did all of this have to happen? Why did these people have to die?

The Governments failed to plan, the citizens failed to take ownership and plan. They didn't know and understand their government.

The Government was all about the business of greed, not protecting the liberty of the people. It is not their job to protect us from ourselves.

They lived with their blinders on and did not stay aware of what was going on with their economy, their personal finances and most importantly their politicians. They always left it up to the "Smart People" to figure things out.

"They will figure it out... they always do." Is their sentiment, and they are ignorant and stupid.

Martin Luther King Jr. said this;

> *"Nothing in the world is more dangerous than sincere ignorance and conscientious stupidity"*

Dr. King is right! You cannot live in ignorance any longer!

You cannot rely on the Government to provide for you.

You must take action and make sure that your family has food and supplies and not comply when they illegally try to take your belongings.

The fourth amendment of the constitutions states;

> *"The right of the people to be secure in their persons, houses, papers, and effects, against unreasonable searches and seizures, shall not be violated, and no Warrants shall issue, but upon probable cause, supported by Oath or affirmation, and particularly describing the place to be searched, and the persons or things to be seized."*

This is your right.

If you're doing something wrong. Expect <u>local law enforcement</u>, not the military to come to your home. But the Military has no right to take your personal belongings not even under executive order.

That is Martial Law and a violation of your rights and constitutional freedoms.

But what if it does happen? What do you do? How do you unlike the man in the story protect your family?

Are you still with me? Are you scared? Are you beginning to think for yourself? Are you willing to do something about it to ensure your families future?

It is time to plan.

Bullets, Beans and Band-Aids...
Where do you start?

Truth # 6 -   How you should prepare your family for the future if we don't fix the system.

We as a nation are reaching the extreme tipping point. We are either going to slide down the slope of an economic collapse in our country or decide that we are no longer going to spend money we don't have and revert back to a precious metals based currency.

But can this really happen? Will the "money power" allow the US to default on its debt and start fresh?

Probably not... and that is why you have to begin to prepare your family for the future!

This chapter is dedicated to making sure that you are ready when the economic collapse happens. Notice I said <u>when, not if</u>. It will come; the money power is too blind to see that they have damaged the economy too badly.

You have to prepare now.

No matter where you are you are in life one fact remains is that you need three things to survive, food, water, and shelter.

As you read in the chapter before, the man in the story didn't really plan ahead. He took a reactive approach to life.

Eventually due to his lack of planning his family will starve and die.

That is a very scary thought for any parent.

Everyone needs to have a plan.

Everyone needs to have food and supplies stored away for any type of emergency be it; natural, economic, or war based crisis.

Naturally as you have read through my past chapters you have begun to feel a strong sense of either two things; panic or inspiration.

You have to act now. If you are feeling that sense of panic, take a deep breath. You are going to be alright! You still have time to plan although be it limited.

If you have felt the inspiration to begin, congratulations you have taken the first step in becoming your own person and learning to not be reliant on government handouts and their control.

So where do you start? This is a very overwhelming feeling. How do you begin planning for your family to have independence once the economy collapses? The easiest way is this; follow the rule of the three b's and focus on;

Beans, Bullets & Bandages

This is the easiest way to help you start to plan for your family for economic fallout.

I'll tell you first how I did it, what tools I used and how I continue to plan for the time when there won't be grocery stores, shopping malls, or sporting outlet stores.

Now, let me preface the following information. There are others who are much, much better than I on how to prepare your family for the un-foreseen. However, I will offer you only what my family has done to be ready for what is coming.

I would encourage you to do your own research, design your own plan and test it.

When I started my prepping in late November of 2011 I first had to look at my budget. Being on a limited budget and in a new job earning less, we had to take a good hard look at what our outgoing expenses were. We eliminated the eating out and the frivolous things. No more quick trips to Target for this thing or the other.

We could no longer afford to be nickel'd and dime'd to death. We lowered our cell phone plans, we eliminated things like Hulu for our TV, Redbox and other entertainment choices were all evaluated on a needs basis. We still have fun with our kids but we have scaled way back.

We looked for ways to use one car instead of two. We use lots of coupons in our shopping; we look for ways to "*bogo*" or buy one get one free. We shop in our bulk section of our local grocery store, we don't buy pre-packaged items. Bulk is always cheaper!

We looked for any excuse to cut money. We found well over $100 a month we could dedicate to prepping our family.

You would be very surprised that when you begin to sacrifice, how much money you can use to protect your family! Once you have this done you can move onto your first of your planning focuses;

1 - Beans

We first started off by looking at our current food supplies. How long could we last with what was in our cupboards?

That was a disturbing reality.

Of what we kept in our pantry and what was in our kitchen we really only had about 5 days worth of food that was consumable. We didn't have enough salt, not enough flour for more than 3 loaves of bread, limited yeast and very limited canned goods, and absolutely no garden.

We needed to know how much we had to have put away. We began to dig through the thousands of websites out there found the following ideas;

There are several schools of thought when it comes to food planning, some say heavy protein, some say garden, some say # 10 cans of dehydrated food. But almost all of them say, keep things you normally eat on hand, do not just buy all dry goods – it is too much of a shock to go from eating normal every day food to freeze dried food. Have a healthy mix of both.

We have a hybrid of all the different plans out there. We have dried goods we bought at the bulk section at our local grocery, we have # 10 cans of dried meat, chicken, soups, and vegetables, we also have planted a sizable bucket garden, that way if we need to leave our current residence and relocate we can take our plants with us.

Your family needs 6 months worth of food to be able to get over the "hump" of the collapse. It would at minimum of three months for some type of organized government structure to emerge, then an additional 2 months possibly for them to get some types of basic services back on line (i.e water, power and lights).

You can put away more food if need be to help your neighbors and family, I would personally strive for 12 months and keep most of it off site if you can.

So, how much does your family need? What do you have in your kitchen that you could live off? Do you have a pantry, if so how much is in it? These are some big questions to ask yourself when you start planning. Do you have space to store your food storage items?

Storage seems to be a bigger problem that we have run into the in past and we have found that under beds works well, backs of closets and stacking 5 gallon buckets in the garage works great.

So, how do you come up with a target for how much your family needs?

There is a website that I love due to the fact that it has a great long term food storage calculator on it. The web site is;

http://foodstoragemadeeasy.net/fsme/docs/
foodstoragecalculator.xls

If you copy and paste or type in this link into any internet browser it will allow you to download a food storage calculator in excel format to your Mac or PC computer that you can use to put estimate how much food and dried goods your family needs.

Once you have an idea of how much you need. I would strongly recommend based on your budget that you aggressively begin to buy and store what you need.

Here is a good rule of thumb, when you store dry goods. Always use good, dry, clean 5 gallon buckets with oxygen absorbers and a very tight lid. Some would say use mylar bags too, but that is up to you.

I keep my dried goods in a dark cool place away from heat or sunlight so I don't worry too much about the breakdown from light.

If you are a parent, feeding your children is the most important step of all. Nothing and I repeat that nothing is more heart breaking than having to tell your children that you have nothing for them to eat.

Imagine looking in to your children's hollow eyes and having to tell them that there is nothing for you to give them. Not only will you have tears to deal with, but their health and safety are now in jeopardy. You didn't plan. You wanted a new pair of shoes, you wanted a bigger boat, you wanted something bigger, better and more expensive and you didn't have the money to plan on food for your kids. <u>Do not let this happen!</u>

When it comes to water, more is better. The recommendation is 1 gallon per member of your household per day for three months. Now I know that I have 6 people in my family so the minimum I need to have on hand 540 gallons of water.

This can present a challenge. But there are very good water filters such as the Berky filter system. Yes, they are pricy but they will be very worth it in the long run.

Here is a stark rule of thumb for you. The rule is 3, 3 & 3. You can only survive when the following conditions are met; 3 minutes without oxygen, 3 days without water, or 3 weeks without food.

Water can be stored in many different forms, Water storage boxes, water storage bricks, and bottled. 50 gallon food safe drums are always an option, but first need to be cleaned. You can use bleach to sanitize water. Here is the Washington State department of Health recommendations for sanitizing bleach;

Treating Water with a 5-6 Percent Liquid Chlorine Bleach Solution		
Volume of Water to be Treated	Treating Clear/Cloudy Water: Bleach Solution to Add	Treating Cloudy, Very Cold, or Surface Water: Bleach Solution to Add
1 quart/1 liter	3 drops	5 drops
1/2 gallon/2 quarts/2 liters	5 drops	10 drops
1 gallon	1/8 teaspoon	1/4 teaspoon
5 gallons	1/2 teaspoon	1 teaspoon
10 gallons	1 teaspoon	2 teaspoons

Once you have your food and water situation at a controllable level you need to turn your attention to cooking and heat.

There are many different forms of cooking, but some of the strongest I have seen have some from solar based ovens and rocket stoves. "Hay" bags are another method of residual heat cooking as well as Dutch oven cooking.

Have some type of cooking option. I would strongly recommend a wood based option due to the ample wood supplies in the Pacific Northwest, but depending on your geographic region you may find that different fuels work better. Most cooking options also provide heat as well and heat is a major factor when it comes to comfort. Most people can take a limited lifestyle as long as they have a heat source to keep them warm and food in their bellies to keep them happy.

Manual cooking devices are also a must and garage sales are a great place to find them. Meat grinders, egg beaters, coffee percolators, hand blenders are all really great ways to get "modern convenience" without having to have power.

Keep yourself healthy and safe; keep your children healthy and safe. Plan ahead! It will require some sacrifices now, but when the bottom falls out on the economy, you will be ready. Don't let your family starve and die!

#2 - Bullets

Guns. Never has there been a more hotly contested subject when it comes to prepping. Some would say that you need to have a huge arsenal; others would say that you need to have just a rifle in the house.

Why do you need to have a gun? Two reasons; to be able to hunt and feed your family, and for the second reason.

Security from others who will hurt or kill your family to take what they need.

In a situation where there are no resources for anyone to find food, water or proper shelter, people begin to justify the most terrible things.

How many times have you told a friend, "I would kill to save my child!" Would you? Could you?

Well guess what? Someone else will too to get what you have. They have a child to save, they have a belly to fill. You cannot risk your family or your supplies.

When the economy declines to such a point that Food Stamps, Social Security and other Government programs are gone, there will be no money to buy food or water. People will come looking for yours. You have to be prepared to let people know that you have to protect your family first, and then maybe, just maybe you can help them.

So… If I have to have a gun, what do I need?

Here is what I would recommend.

Start with the right type of gun. Start small first. Most people have never handled a firearm before so I would start with a .22 caliber rifle.

Buy it new.

Buy one with a synthetic stock and an extended magazine. Find a place that you can shoot it and practice, practice, practice. .22 ammunition is cheap and easy to find. This will help you to understand the mechanics of a gun and how to properly shoot it. Get 1000 rounds for it.

Next find a forest full of squirrels, chipmunks or bigger birds and kill one. What?? You want me to kill something? Yes, I want you to kill something with it. You have to get over the whole "Gods precious creatures" thing and kill an animal.

The initial shock of knowing that you have killed an animal will be tough but you have to learn to break through the mental barriers of taking an animals life.

When you learn what to do, it will help you react better when the time comes and you have to start hunting on a more full time basis to feed your family.

Next, buy a handgun. I would recommend a magazine based model with a slide action. Any gun .45, 9mm or .32 caliber or more should be sufficient to protect you from anyone who gets too close.

Yes, I said <u>anyone</u>.

This gun is for your personal safety security. The handgun was invented for one purpose. To kill people. Sure, you could kill an animal with it if you really needed but if someone is coming into your home or approaching you with the intent to take your food or your life you need to be ready to do the unthinkable. Buy 1000 rounds for this weapon.

Nothing matters more in this world than your family. Nothing. You have to be ready to stop the person who would hurt your kids and take the food that you have worked so hard to have ready for them. You may even have to stop rouge police officers or soldiers who wouldn't think twice about killing you and your family to take your supplies for the "greater good". You have read the executive orders and heard what could happen. Do not be a victim.

The final two guns I would recommend would be a .12 gauge shotgun and a large hunting or assault rifle. These two are designed for hunting animals, and some level of personal security.

The .12 gauge can shot different loads of bird shot shells and slugs based ammo. It is mostly used to hunt birds such as duck, turkey quail or grouse.

I would strongly recommend talking to your local sporting goods store gun department manager to understand what type of load you should use to hunt what type of fowl. Buy a mix of rounds for this gun I would recommend 200 of each for a total of 1000 rounds.

The final weapon is up for debate. Having a hunting rifle .270 caliber or bigger or an assault rifle both can help you hunt large game such as bear, moose, elk or deer but having just the hunting rifle can be a good thing. It can double as a long range fighting gun but an assault rifle also works for that too.

If you're going to buy an assault rifle I would recommend an AK-47. It is a reliable gun and they are readily available to find. It was designed to run under the most unfriendly conditions known to man. Parts are easy to get as well as ammunition.

Some gun scholars think the AR-15 is a better weapon. They both have their ups and downs and on this one you have to decide for yourself. Consult your local army surplus store and ask their opinion of what weapon is better.

Once you have your hunting and defensive weapons it is time to look at your home.

When the time comes you are going to want to eliminate your home as a target. Find a way to black out all of your windows. Crowds and looters are drawn to lighted places. Where there is light there are people, and where there are people there is food and water or supplies.

Figure out a way to re-enforce your doors. One of the most basic ways is a backstop design or front door security is a security bar. Windows can be re-enforced with a heat shrink wrap to prevent a hammer blow, or my strong recommendation, pre-cut wood to match all of your window sizes.

Keep some money on hand, mainly silver coin and small bars. Silver is the most negotiable form of currency when the paper stuff we use is no longer valid.

As you have read, silver and gold were our currency of choice during the American Revolution and should our current paper currency become nothing more than glorified scratch paper it will be the most effective ways for you to barter for services and food. Coming from a Banker, silver is the most flexible currency you can have on hand.

I would keep a full tool box on each level of your home for quick access to tools and keep a gas wrench near you gas shut off valve just in case. If a natural disaster occurs and breaks your gas line, you will want to shut it off right away.

Your home is your castle and most people do not own additional property that they could retreat to incase of economic collapse or martial law. Take care of your home and prepare it, and it will be your fortress to keep you safe when the time comes.

Get a generator – one big enough to just meet your family's needs. I have included a estimation charge below so you can see what items in your home use;

	Approximate Starting Wattage (what is this?)	Approximate Running Wattage(what is this?)	240V required?
Refrigerator or Freezer (Energy Star)	1200	132–192	
Microwave Oven			
650 watts	1000	1000	
800 watts	1300	1300	
1000 watts	1500	1500	
Incandescent Lights	as indicated on bulb (i.e. 60W)	as indicated on bulb (i.e 60W)	
Furnace Fan, gas or fuel oil			
1/8 Horsepower	500	300	Y
1/6 Horsepower	750	500	Y
1/4 Horsepower	1000	600	Y
1/3 Horsepower	1400	700	Y
1/2 Horsepower	2350	875	Y
Television			
Tube type	300	300	
Flat Screen (20")	120	120	
Flat Screen (46")	190	190	
Coffee Maker (4 cup)	600	600	
Dishwasher (Cool Dry)	540	216	
Electric Fry Pan	1500	1500	
Electric Range (8-inch element)	2100	2100	Y
Automatic Washer	1200	1200	

	Approximate Starting Wattage (what is this?)	Approximate Running Wattage(what is this?)	240V required?
Clothes Dryer (Electric)	6750	5400	Y
Radio	50 to 200	50 to 200	
Sump Pump			
1/3 Horsepower	1300	800	Y
1/2 Horsepower	2150	1050	Y
Window Air Conditioner (10,000 BTU)	2200	1500	
Computer			
Laptop	200–250	200–250	
Desktop	600–800	600–800	
Monitor (LCD style)	30	30	
Printer	400–600	400–600	
Hot Water Heater	4500	4500	Y
Garage Door Opener	1420	720	

You can store fuel to help with your generator but I would strongly recommend looking up your local state and county codes on fuel storage. Personally I believe you should store what you need and that no county and state regulations should limit what you can and cannot store. They may say it is for their protection, but more or less it is for their control of your fuel supply.

#3 – Band-aids

First aid is one of the biggest and most important parts of learning to prepare your family for disaster. What would happen if someone got cut badly? Could you handle blood? Do you have the tools and supplies to stop someone from dying? Do you have a person in your home who is diabetic? Disabled? What would you do?

Any parent should sit up and pay very close attention to this particular section. Your children are your future, and their health and welfare come before yours in all situations. If one of them were to become injured, how would you help them? Get first aid certified today.

Get CPR certified today as well. Here is the phone number for the American Red Cross;

1-877-272-7337

Call them and get scheduled in a class today. The other item you will want to have on hand is a very comprehensive first aid kit. This will cost you some money, however if you visit your local Walmart you can stock up on just about everything you need at a better rate. Pre-fab kits are nice to have but in the long run you can save more money by building your own first aid kit. Here is what the web site www.kidshealth.org recommends;

- first-aid manual

- sterile gauze pads of different sizes

- adhesive tape

- adhesive bandages in several sizes

- elastic bandage

- a splint for both fingers, arms and ankles.

- antiseptic wipes

- soap

- antibiotic ointment

- antiseptic solution (like hydrogen peroxide)

- Hydrocortisone cream (1%)

- acetaminophen and ibuprofen

- extra prescription medications (if the family is going on vacation)

- tweezers

- sharp scissors

- safety pins

- disposable instant cold packs

- calamine lotion

- alcohol wipes or ethyl alcohol

- thermometer

- plastic non-latex gloves (at least 2 pairs)

- flashlight and extra batteries

- a blanket

- mouthpiece for administering CPR (can be obtained from your local Red Cross)

- your list of emergency phone numbers

- blanket (stored nearby)

- Insulin (for diabetics)

You can add more or less of the items depending on what your family's needs are, however I am not an expert in health, contact your local chapter of the Red Cross to discuss with them what should be in your kit.

But regardless of the cost of putting the kit together you should have one. Remember your sacrifices mean something down the road. Being prepared for first aid is a key to survival. You can always hope for the best for your family but you need to be prepared

I have only skimmed the surface in this chapter about being prepared and being ready when the coming collapse happens. I hope that as you have read through this that you have begun formulating a game plan on how you are going to make sure that your family is protected.

Rise Up Now or Fall Down Forever!

"The tree of liberty must be refreshed from time to time with the blood of patriots and tyrants."

Thomas Jefferson

Truth #7 -   **Finally what we as citizens need to do - rise up and act now or we will fall down and never be able to rise again!**

Revolution.

It is a very, very dangerous word. It brings fear into the heart of the unprepared man and causes the powerful elite to lose sleep, panic and implement martial law to grasp at the strings of their false power.

A new revolution is brewing! The people are beginning to wake up! In one form or another revolution is coming!

There is a great song by the singer Phil Collins; the song is, "In the AirTonight." The lyrics are strangely eerie of what is taking place right now in the world. It states;

> *"I can feel it coming I the air tonight, oh Lord,*
> *And I've been waiting for this moment for all my life,*
> *Can you feel it coming in the air tonight?"*

Can you feel the tension in the air in this country? Can you feel that what you have read and what you now know about our Government and Financial system is true and will cause our destruction?

But one very large question remains... what type of revolution will we have?

Will *"We The People"* be able to get our Politicians to finally listen to us and make the hard choices to eliminate what we borrow from the corrupt Federal Reserve and rely on our own tax dollars and income to run our country?

Or will we enter into a true civil war. The Department of Homeland Security is ready for it. They bought 1.2 million rounds of hollow point ammunition in March of 2012.

Will millions have to die to form a new nation? Will the most innocent among us, children bear the brunt of the burden of war and loose Moms and Dads? Will we have fight brother against brother as we did over one hundred years ago?

Wake up O America, and see what is happening in Greece and in Spain! It can be avoided! We can get past this without a drop of blood shed!

But *"We the People"* will have to learn to get beyond ourselves! We will have to get beyond our Coach hand bags, our IPhones, our clothes, our homes our cars, our welfare, our SSI payment, our own depression, our ... stuff!

We will have to let it all go and find common ground in what we will need to bind together for, our survival as a country! If we continue to live in a world of taking hand outs and wanting to take from country that many died to protect we will fail miserably!

We have to act together in one voice and one mind.

Of a mind and heart dedicated to God, and country and to tell our elected officials that enough is enough, we need get back to the constitution, smaller government, and less infringement on our personal liberties.

Yes, do I believe in Gods law and the marvelous things that it can do for us! My faith plays an important part in my life!

But this this not what I have written about!

I am writing to wake you up! I am writing to get you to realize the world around you is in danger,

I am writing to you in the hopes that what you have read in this book will inspire you to take pride in our nation, and in your life and your future!

Please, please for the sake of our children's futures stop what you are doing!

We have to become a nation of people who take ownership of their problems, not a nation who believes in blaming other countries for our problems. Who sits back and says, "someone else will take care of it..."

Our Politicians do it all the time! They blame each other!

We have to seize control of our future as a nation and fix the issues with our national debt! We inherit the America of tomorrow!

You now have to make a choice. What side will you be on?

Will you continue to languish in the mire of mediocrity?

Will you continue to take handouts and rely on a system that will fail very soon?

Will you give up your freedoms as an American and allow the Government to control who you are, where you go, how you do it and eventually how you will say it?

NO!

Rise up I say!

Tell your elected officials that enough is enough. We want to have a nation to celebrate! Tell them to cut the spending, and only rely on the tax income we have and end the relationship and charter of the Federal Reserve Bank!

Tell them to go back to a Gold or Silver backed currency!

Tell them that the current paper currency we have is illegal and should be replaced with gold and silver!

Tell them that if they don't represent you fairly and accurately that they will not get your vote!

Tell them with your voices, and with your actions! Write letters to your state representatives! Discuss the issues with family and friends, you could also take ownership and run for office!

Get your voice to mean something! Give your words purpose!

Because if you don't have your voice to mean something, someone else may say something else but they may do it with violence!

They will rebel and speak for you! They will do something in the name of "greater good" that is only for anarchy! Not for the good of anyone!

Prepare for your family! Prepare with beans, bullets and band-aids! If the worst comes, do not let your family suffer! Be the provider that God wants you to be for your family!

I will close with this;

One of my favorite versus in the bible is in Proverbs 22:3 -

"A prudent man sees danger and take refuge, but the simple keep going and suffer for it!"

See the danger coming. Hide yourself and prepare your family for it! Hopefully my words have inspired you to accomplish something so much greater!

Be aware, watch around you and tell others when something doesn't feel right!

May God bless and provide for you in your new journey!

Dear Reader

Thank you for reading "The Red Pill". I hope you found it informative and inspiring to get your family ready for the coming economic collapse.

If you found this book woke you up, please pass it to a family or friend. My goal in writing this book was to wake up as many hearts and minds in an effort to pull families together, help them prepare and possibly redirect their hearts back to God.

Please consider your family and friends as you read this book. Be brave, trust in God and pass the truth along!

www.ingramcontent.com/pod-product-compliance
Lightning Source LLC
Chambersburg PA
CBHW022131170526
45157CB00004B/1836